Note to parents, carers and teachers

Read it yourself is a series of modern stories, favourite characters, traditional tales and first reference books written in a simple way for children who are learning to read. The books can be read independently or as part of a guided reading session.

Each book is carefully structured to include many high-frequency words vital for first reading. The sentences on each page are supported closely by pictures to help with understanding, and to offer lively details to talk about.

The books are graded into four levels that progressively introduce wider vocabulary and longer text as a reader's ability and confidence grows.

Ideas for use

- Ask how your child would like to approach reading at this stage. Would he prefer to hear you read the book first, or would he like to read the words to you and see how he gets on?

- Help him to sound out any words he does not know.

- Developing readers can be concentrating so hard on the words that they sometimes don't fully grasp the meaning of what they're reading. Answering the quiz questions at the end of the book will help with understanding.

For more information and advice on Read it yourself and book banding, visit www.ladybird.com/readityourself

Book
Band
7

Level 3 is ideal for children who are developing reading confidence and stamina, and who are eager to read longer books with a wider vocabulary.

Special features:

Detailed pictures for added interest and discussion

Wider vocabulary, reinforced through repetition

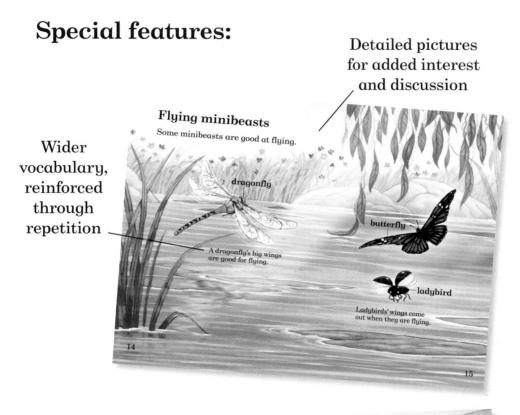

Flying minibeasts

Some minibeasts are good at flying.

dragonfly

A dragonfly's big wings are good for flying.

butterfly

ladybird

Ladybirds' wings come out when they are flying.

14

15

Longer sentences

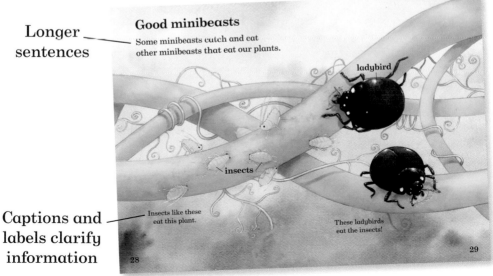

Good minibeasts

Some minibeasts catch and eat other minibeasts that eat our plants.

ladybird

insects

Insects like these eat this plant.

These ladybirds eat the insects!

Captions and labels clarify information

28

29

Educational Consultant: Geraldine Taylor
Book Banding Consultant: Kate Ruttle
Subject Consultant: Dr Kim Dennis-Bryan

LADYBIRD BOOKS

UK | USA | Canada | Ireland | Australia
India | New Zealand | South Africa

Ladybird Books is part of the Penguin Random House group of companies
whose addresses can be found at global.penguinrandomhouse.com.

www.penguin.co.uk   www.puffin.co.uk   www.ladybird.co.uk

Penguin
Random House
UK

First published 2016
This edition 2019
002

Copyright © Ladybird Books Ltd, 2016

Printed in China

A CIP catalogue record for this book is available from the British Library

ISBN: 978–0–241–40540–6

All correspondence to:
Ladybird Books
Penguin Random House Children's
One Embassy Gardens, 8 Viaduct Gardens, London SW11 7BW

Minibeasts

Written by Chris Baker
Illustrated by Daniel Howarth

Contents

Minibeasts are little

Minibeasts are very little creatures.
They live in many different places.

on plants

in a pond

Minibeasts live
in all these places.

on old food

underground

Insects are minibeasts

Insects are minibeasts that have six legs. There are many different kinds of insect.

ant

ladybird

bee

butterfly

water boatman

Other minibeasts

Not all minibeasts have six legs like insects do. Minibeasts can have different kinds of bodies.

centipede

spider

snail

How many legs does the spider have?

Flying minibeasts

Some minibeasts are good at flying.

dragonfly

A dragonfly's big wings
are good for flying.

butterfly

ladybird

Ladybirds' wings come
out when they are flying.

15

Water minibeasts

Some minibeasts can live
and swim in water.

Water boatmen and pond
snails live in ponds.

A water boatman swims
in the water with its legs.

**water
boatman**

**pond
snail**

Under the ground

Some minibeasts live under the ground in nests. Many ants live in nests that they dig underground, but they come out to get food.

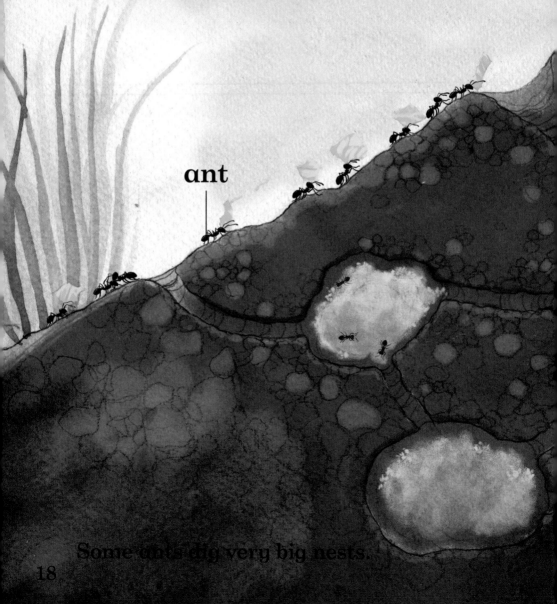

ant

Some ants dig very big nests.

Look how big this nest is!

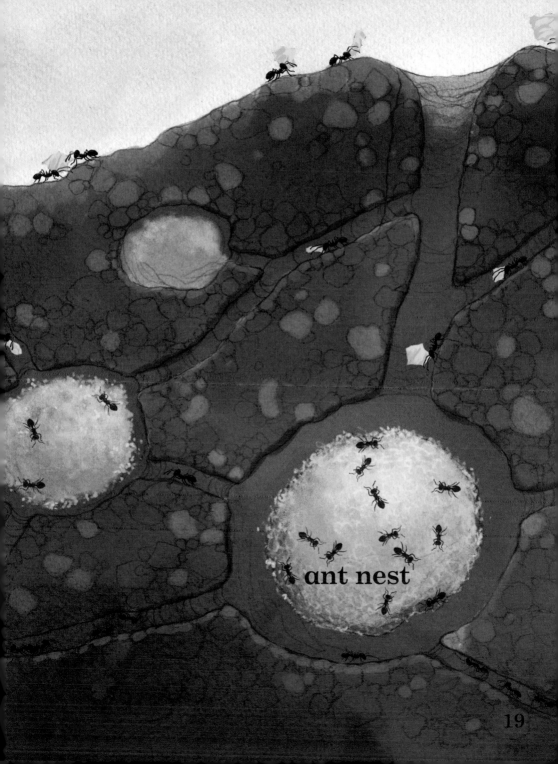

ant nest

Snails

Minibeasts eat many different things. Snails eat plants.

garden snail

Some snails live in gardens.

Some snails live in ponds.

pond snail

Pond snails eat plants in the water.

Minibeasts clear up!

Some minibeasts eat old food, and other old things too. They help clear up our gardens.

Some minibeasts help clear up our food!

old food

Centipedes

Some minibeasts catch and eat
their food. Centipedes eat many
kinds of other little creatures.

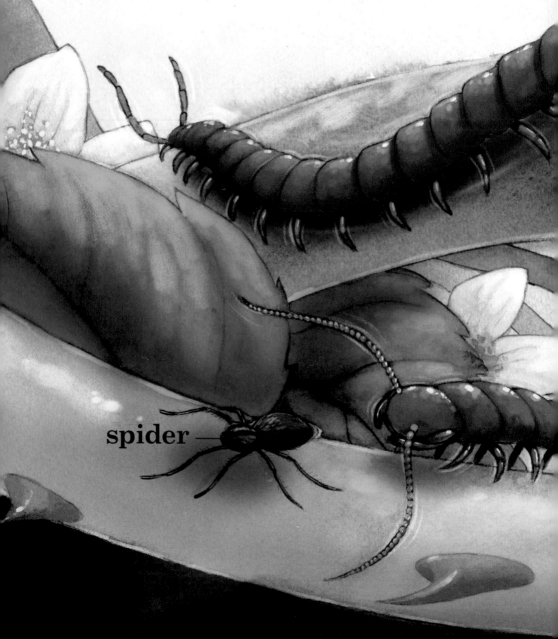

spider

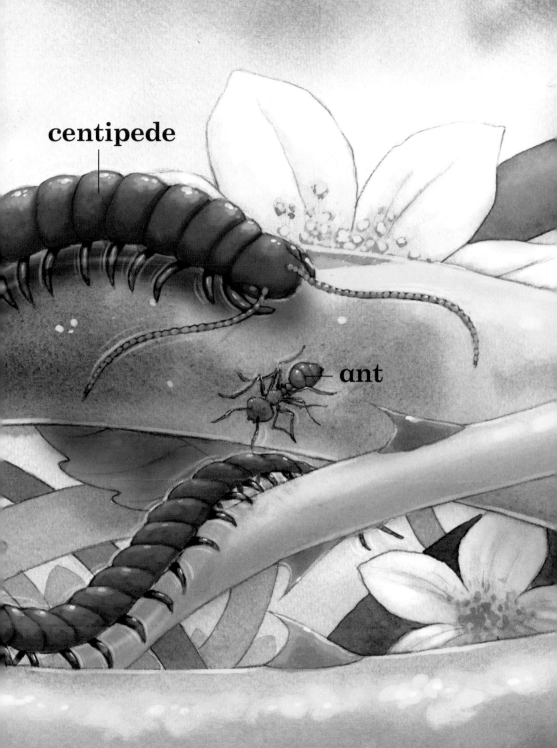

centipede

ant

Centipedes catch and eat other
minibeasts, like ants and spiders.

Spiders

Some spiders make webs to catch other minibeasts.

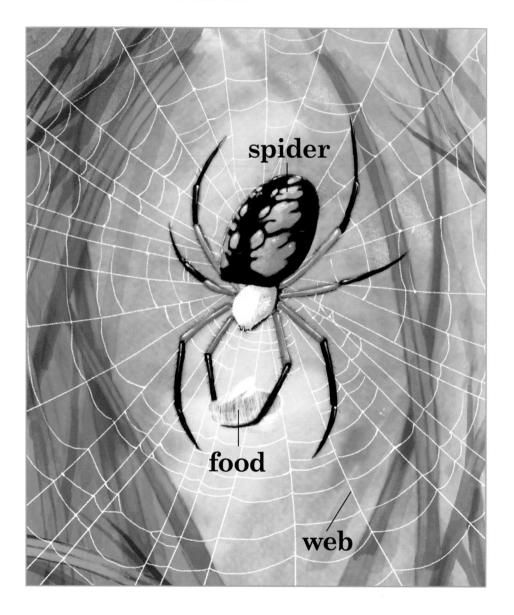

Spiders can make webs to catch their food.

Other spiders can run fast to catch food.

tarantula

food

This tarantula runs fast to catch food.

Good minibeasts

Some minibeasts catch and eat other minibeasts that eat our plants.

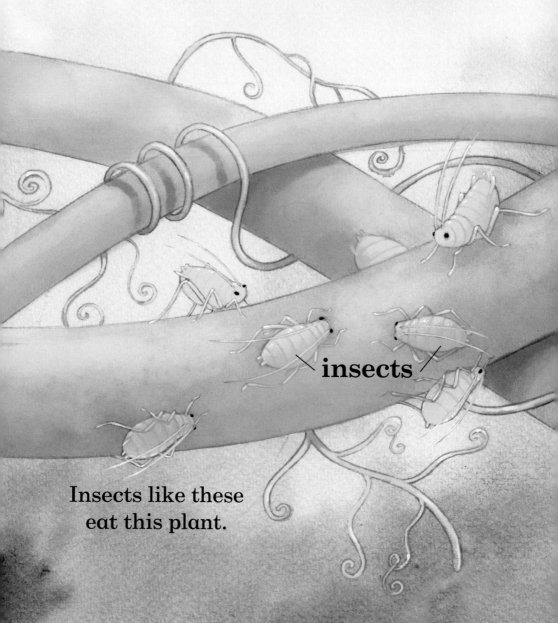

insects

Insects like these eat this plant.

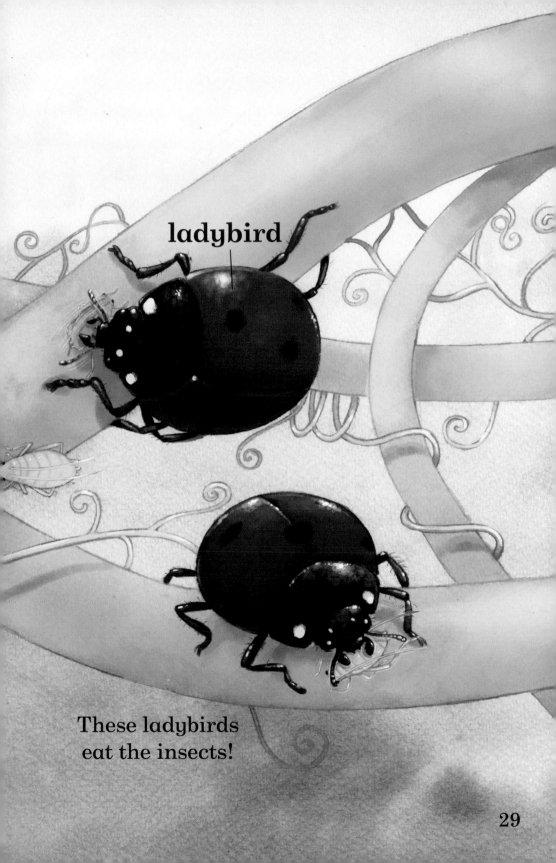

ladybird

These ladybirds
eat the insects!

29

Bees help

Some minibeasts help plants grow fruits.

1 The bee is on this flower to get food.

pollen

2 The pollen can get on the bee.

3 Bees take pollen to other flowers.
The pollen helps flowers to make fruits.

Little minibeasts

Minibeasts come out of eggs.
Some minibeasts look much like
the adults when they come out.

an egg

1 First, it is an egg.

2 Then, it is a little spider.

They have to grow, but their
bodies do not change very much.

3 Then, it is an adult spider.

Egg to butterfly

Butterflies come out of eggs, but they are caterpillars first. Then the caterpillars change into butterflies!

1 An egg

2 A larva

A butterfly larva is called a caterpillar.

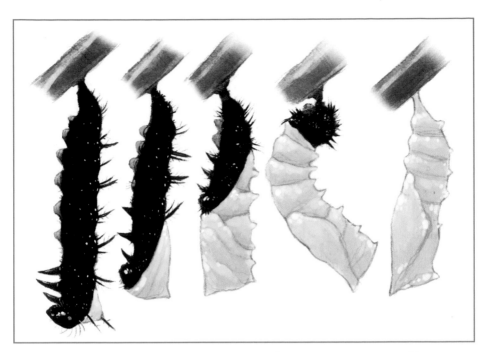

3 A caterpillar changes to a chrysalis.

4 An adult butterfly comes out of the chrysalis!

Bees

Like a butterfly, a bee is first an egg, and then a larva.

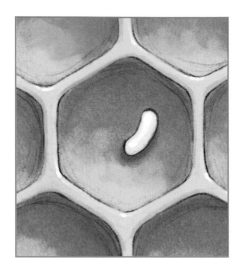

1 An egg

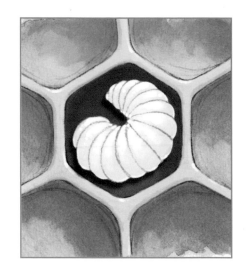

2 A larva

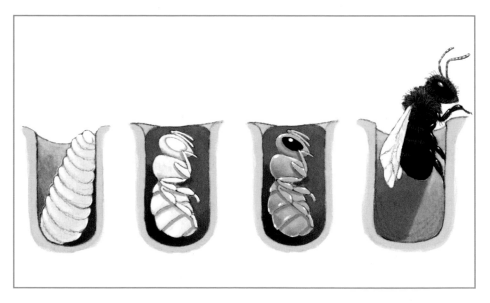

3 The larva changes to an adult

Adult bees live in a nest.

Minibeasts we don't like

Do you love minibeasts? There are some minibeasts we don't like.

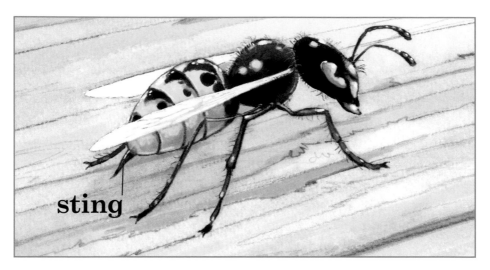

sting

Some minibeasts can sting.

germs

Some minibeasts can get germs on our food.

Some minibeasts eat our food.

Minibeasts we love

But there are some minibeasts we love because they help us.

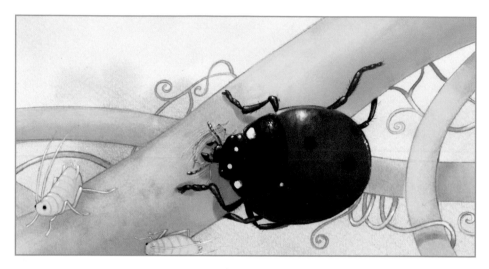

Some minibeasts eat insects we don't like.

Some minibeasts can clear up our food.

Some minibeasts make food.

Looking at minibeasts

You can catch minibeasts to look at them, but you must put them back.

Don't catch minibeasts that sting!

It is good to catch different kinds
of minibeasts and look at them.

Picture glossary

 ant

 bee

 butterfly

 caterpillar

 centipede

 chrysalis

 ladybird

 larva

 snail

 spider

 water boatman

 web

Index

Minibeasts quiz

What have you learnt about minibeasts?
Answer these questions and find out!

- How many legs do insects have?

- Where does a water boatman live?

- Which minibeasts make webs?

- How do some minibeasts help us?

- What does a caterpillar turn into?

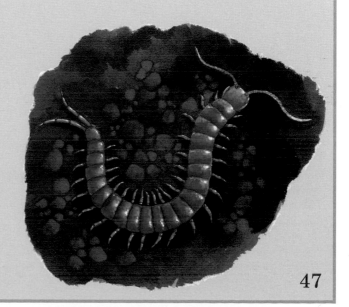

www.ladybird.com